Dedication

"AUNTIE AT THE WEDDING"

is a journey through life and a journey I couldn't have taken without all those who loved and believed in me, you know who are. Although, for this first anthology I will point out my sisters Nikki and Louise; my children Taro and Libby; Teresa my very patient mother, and Michael my late father.

Acknowledgement

I also wish to thank Steve, Vicky, Barbara, Belinda, Carole, Robert, Harula, Tim and Shelley for the support in making an idea a physical entity. Sarah and Restless Theatre CIC for taking a chance on me.

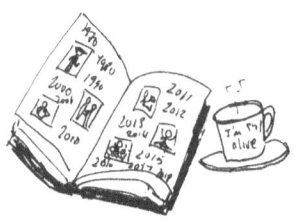

Enna

Email: enna@restlesstheatre.co.uk

ISBN - 978-1-6671-2017-1

Contents

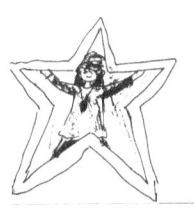

Auntie at the Wedding

There's an Auntie at the wedding
Who's not quite sure why she is there,
But the sherry is flowing freely,
So, she doesn't really care.

She knows she's related to someone,
The bride or groom – one of the two.
She thinks it's through her estranged brother,
Who has several children – some she knew.

She doesn't really know anyone,
But it was nice to be invited.
Gave her an excuse to wear a fascinator,
And the chance to get excited.

Her brother is here somewhere,
They haven't spoken for many years.
The bride apparently didn't like that,
Her invitation was sent with tears.

There is nothing like a family wedding,
To dig up relics of the past.
Aunty may wonder though,
If this should be her last.

Stuck at a table of random relatives,
Or friends or someone with an obscure link
To the celebrating newlyweds
Still, there is certainly plenty to drink.

Later, slightly pickled in a corner,
Watching the youngsters dance…
"Aunty Grace! I thought it was you!
Thanks for helping celebrate my romance!"

With fascinator slipping rakishly over one eye,
It's quite hard to focus on the vision in white.
Not easy to communicate with glass half empty,
And wondering how you'll get home tonight.

"Oh, my dear, what a lovely wedding."
She manages, as the room begins to spin.
"I do hope you'll both be happy."
The bride continues to grin.

It's clear that both Aunty and the bride,
Have had quite a few.
Aunty is very pleased to see her,
But begins to wish she would move.

The room is spinning more now,
And other things are brewing.
'Please beautiful bride, whoever you are,
Move quickly before I start spewing.'

She doesn't say this out loud of course,
That would really be quite rude.
But what might happen next will be worse,
She wishes she hadn't eaten so much food.

Lucky for her (and the bride)
She's spared, as the groom appears.
"Gav, this is great aunty Grace. I used to visit her place."
"Charmed to meet you my dears."

She thinks 'oh please delightful couple,
Get away from me,
Things will get unpleasant here,
If only you could see.

Then another person appears
Looks like it could be her brother Pat,
"Hey, is that you Gracie?
I really like the hat."

Bride and groom are suddenly distracted,
By a call over the P.A.
"Let's have the lovely couple in the centre,
And give them a hip hip hooray!"

Grace manages to blurt out an apology,
To her brother and nips to the loo.
Things seem so much better here,
Even if she has an unpleasant view.

Returning to the party
Hoping soon to go home,
It appears her misdemeanour,
Was undetected – and she was not alone.

A bit of a catastrophe has occurred.
Which will challenge the love in the room.
Tears and people bustling, rushing around,
The bride has thrown up on the groom.

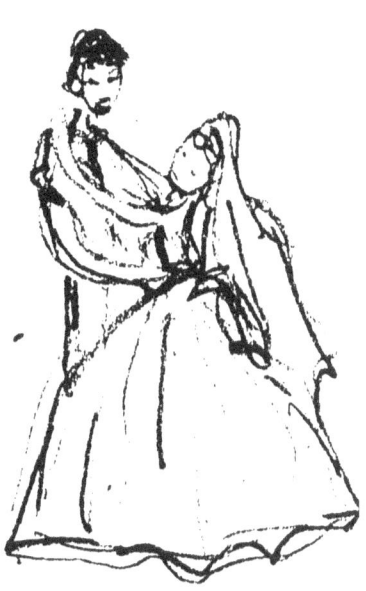

As things calm down, Pat reappears,
"I missed you sister dear,
Hopefully, we'll see you again,
At the Christening next year."

Grace thanks her brother kindly
Yet so much is left unsaid.
They haven't talked in years,
And the closeness of the past seems dead.

They turn to look at each other.
With a matching pair of eyes.
They don't know what to say anymore,
But suddenly a surprise.

Gales of unprovoked laughter
From Grace and her brother too.
He says "I think my granddaughter,
Is very much like you."

The laughter peals away the layers
Of over 50 years.
Another family wedding,
Another lot of tears.

When Grace got married to her beau
A lovely man named Hugh.
He sadly died many years ago,
As a bride – she threw up on him too.

A very merry wedding day
With family love abound…
She nursed her husband until the end,
Her brother beside her, as Hugh was put into the ground.

Yes, true love can stand the test of time.
Unexpected vomiting won't get in the way,
And family can always be there for you.
Even if you have nothing to say.

So, Aunty recalls this wedding,
As much as she remembers hers.
Things don't always go to plan,
But they can be oh, so much worse.

She files away the memories,
As she puts the fascinator away.
Maybe she'll get it out again,
And this time she'll have more to say.

She writes a thank you letter,
Always polite is Aunty G.
She may be invited, she may get excited,
But next time she'll stick to tea.

Looking at the photographs
Showing many an aging face.
Making room for so many more
Yet her wedding picture has pride of place.

Aunty Grace is not forgotten,
Though her life now seems so tame.
Within the age lines is a smile
Of a girl with passion lit aflame.

The aunty at the wedding
Not many know her name,
But take the time to talk to her,
And enjoy the riches you could gain.

*(Dedicated to all the elderly aunties who get
invited to family gatherings – even if they can't recall the main participants.)*

Balloons

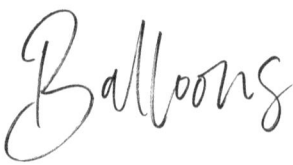

I see a hot air balloon,
Floating in the sky
They always make me,
Think of things,
I don't know why.

It's just a piece of
Inflated material after all
Rising above the clouds.
It's the freedom, I suppose,
From the rat race, the chaos, the crowds

But they always make me think of things,
Don't ask me why.
Though I can imagine
Being in one
Floating above the sky ….

(First published in the anthology Body and Soul by United Press, 2005)

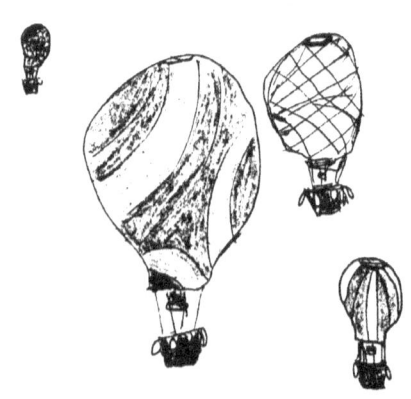

Grans Place

Photographs of when we were young.
On the sideboard, on the wall.
Mementos of the past, in the lounge
In the kitchen and in the hall.

Postcards in the letter rack
From 'way back when'
Mixed with forgotten bills and old letters,
Bringing together now and then.

A dusty cabinet containing trophies,
Won in 'days gone by'.
Open fire, patterned carpet
I look around and sigh,

A contented sigh, for this place
My Gran's home of old
Where she provides warmth and cheer
An oasis in a world so cold.

(Dedicated to my grandmother, Lillian known as Winifred)

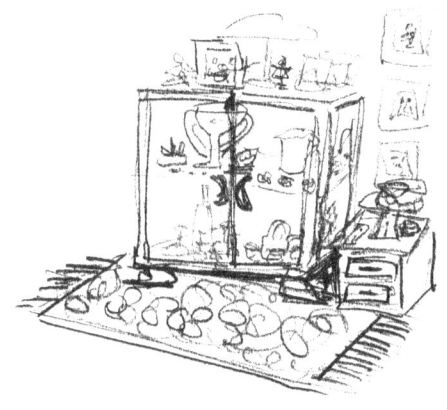

Chocolate Frogs

They're amazing these places,
Known as railway stations.
The café has a life of its own.
Seeing all the nomads
From different destinations
Hurrying by with no time to moan.
About the price of coffee
The condition of the food
About each misleading sign
About an atmosphere like a vacuum
And the latest excuse
"We're so sorry, there's a leaf on the line."
Facing yet another door/machine/platform
Bearing "Sorry not in use…
Normal service as soon as we are able."
I will be 'Getting there' eventually.
Meantime, I gaze at the spilt liquid,
And draw a chocolate frog on the table.

(Written at Birmingham New Street Station, approximately 1992)

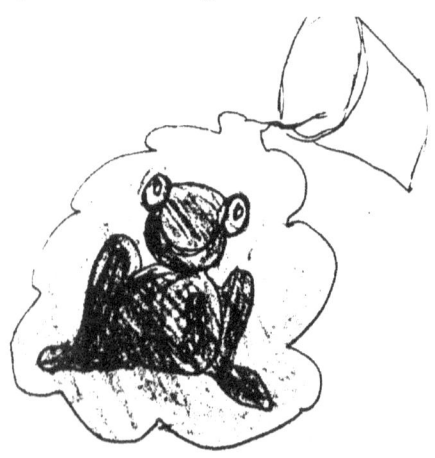

Chips with Everything

Got chatted up in the chip shop again today,
By a bloke with a Scottish lilt.
I pop in there quite often now,
He'll say… .... "D'you want sauce with that?"
I feel as if me heart will melt.

Been here a week now, nice place innit?
Love the beach.
We haven't got one where I live.
Well, you don't usually find them in King's Heath.

Yeah, he was quite nice, this chip shop bloke,
But then everyone is, down here.
Perhaps it's summat they put in the cider.
Certainly, can't be in the beer.

I think I'll pop in again.
I might learn his name.
Who knows, I might have a chance.
Of a holiday romance.
Or a few extra chips.

Pity I've only got a week left.
I could always move down here, he has.
Bugger all in Kings Heath.

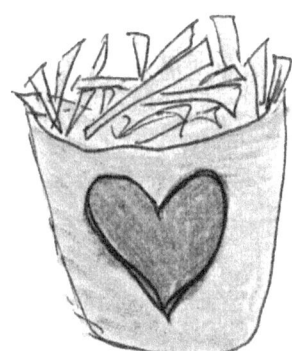

Walking a Hatstand Around Paignton

So, I've missed the bus, no need to fuss,
There will be another along in a minute.
I can just sit and wait and contemplate,
And test my patience to the limit.

I could stop the talk, go for a walk,
Somewhere nice – perhaps the beach.
Wander a bit ... avoid the dog ...muck.
Allow my mind to expand, to reach...

New heights... that would be grand,
But I've got this hatstand.
A special offer from Argos – along the strand.
It's a bit of a liability to carry by hand.

It's not exactly light, but it feels just right,
And at least I can carry it without too much might.
Waiting for buses is a bore,
I need to go to the shore; I can't wait any more.

Yet how to carry such a lot
Of unnecessarily large box
Which I'm certain is mainly packaging
In case the cheap varnished wood faces damaging

It's an hour until the next bus, but I'm bored…
So bored – I can't stand to be so moored.
Therefore, despite the annoying bulk,
And amused looks of the local hulk

Page 14

I go, I go for a little wander, a little ponder.
To see the sea and all its wonder.
With hatstand beside me I breath in the soft salty air.
And at this time of year, I don't have to share…

The beach with anyone but dog walkers
And those who know about the local talkers.
It's my favourite time of year,
When the tourists disappear

I take a moment to accept my situation,
As I dream of sailing off to another nation
With all its mysteries and anticipation.
Yet it's time to get back to the bus station.

I take a moment to reflect on how much I can connect,
As I stand in a queue to board – I'm on next.
I settle comfortably in my seat,
Take out my music, rest my weary feet.

Quite a day it has been and one I'm glad I didn't miss,
Taking a moment to enjoy the peace and acknowledge the bliss…
Of knowing my dreams are well within reach.
Until I remember I left the hatstand on the ruddy beach…

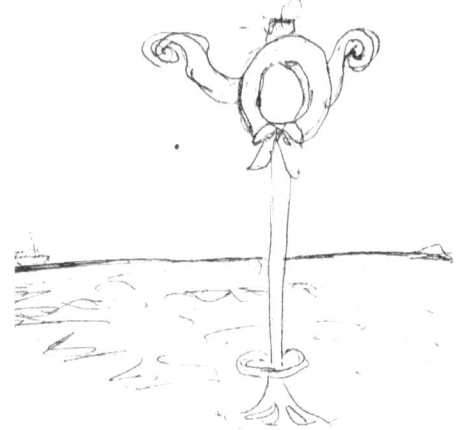

*(This actually happened whilst I was a student –
luckily, I got off the bus in time.)*

Tuesday

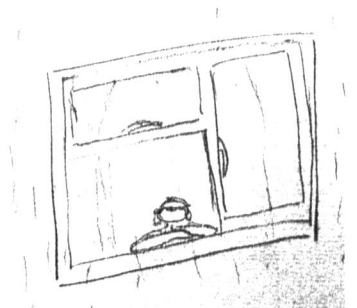

'April Showers' they sing about
But I don't feel like dancing.
It's wet, it's cold. I'm all alone,
And not in any mood for romancing.
It's one of those days, with time to think,
But leaves you with little to say.
The rain, the mood, the nothing-to-do
It has to be Tuesday.

Marmalade

Today has been so bad and it's only just begun.
I'd rather have rainclouds to block the morning sun.
Miss the bus to work, got my breakfast late,
Cannot decide what to put on my plate,
But worse than that… there's a butterknife in the marmalade jar.

Living without you seemed so bad,
But living with you is twice as mad.
I never dreamed it would be this way.
What a start to a 'fantastic' day.

Sometimes the power of one is greater than the power of two,
Sometimes the sun needs to shine alone…
And the marmalade tastes better on its own.

I couldn't bathe because you were there,
Delicately pulling out your nasal hair.
You're very tidy, but obsessively so
And there are some things you don't seem to know,

Like to upset me… Put a butterknife in the marmalade jar.
Living without you caused me pain,
But living with you is driving me insane.
Instead of support, you just get in my way,
What a start to a 'fantastic' day.

Sometimes the power of one is greater than the power of two.
Sometimes the sun needs to shine alone…
And the marmalade tastes better on its own.

I find that there are times when I wish you dead,
Like when your football socks stain my Wonderbra red
And I still can't decide if it was my wish,
To have the nightly fight over the satellite dish
And if I ever said, about the butterknife in the marmalade jar.

Living without you seemed so free,
Living with you, loses me,
But now I can't let you get away,
What a start to a fantastic day.

Sometimes the power of one is increased by the power of two,
Sometimes rain helps the sun to shine brighter… (Brighter)

Sometimes the power of one needs the love and the power of two.
Sometimes you make the sun shine brighter…
And the marmalade tastes better with you.

(Just don't use the butterknife.)

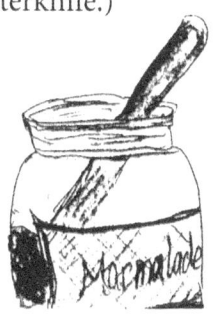

(Imagining a calypso beat when singing.)

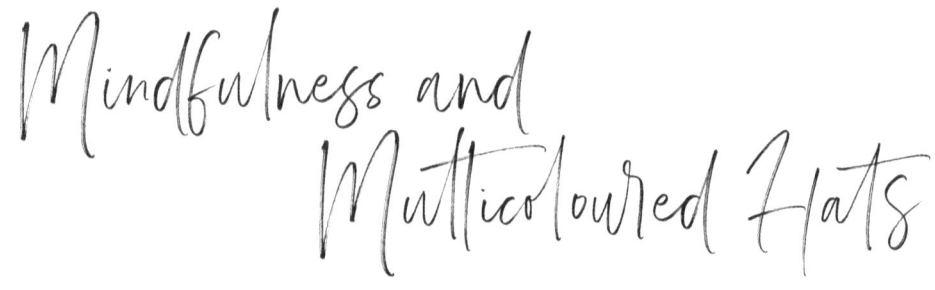

Mindfulness and Multicoloured Hats

I'm making a hat …a multicoloured hat.
It's my exercise in that curious concept and modern byword,
Known as 'mindfulness'.

Yes, you have to be very 'mindful' in making a hat… a multicoloured hat.
Using the best wool my money can buy (about £1.50 a ball).
And a loom I got from a charity shop.

Mindfulness is all about focussing the mind,
Shutting out the chatter, developing focus
Destroying confusion.

Or so I'm led to believe.
Mindfulness should take all your attention and reduce the tension,
Leading to 'stress relief'.

That's why I'm making a hat…a multicoloured hat.

It's not so bad and I'm quite glad when I get to end of it.
It looks fairly nice and you wouldn't think twice,
That stress and anxiety forced me to do it.

Yes, it does provide some relief,
And settles any grief,
About a lack of productivity brought on by depression.

The texture of each hat is soft,
The colours oft… cheer me up.
(Terrible rhyming there, I know … but I don't care.)

So, I'm applying a little time to a mindful activity…
To take some of the stress of the day.
And work towards putting my head in a better space, a better place…

(And one that keeps it quite warm too).

Where hopefully a sense of calm will prevail
And the anxiety will disappear and sail… away for evermore.

A simple activity, now I know how to make these… lovely multicoloured hats.
My exercise in mindfulness and quite a pleasant chore.
To put stress in its place once more.

What to do with them once made, I am just not sure...
At the moment, I believe there are more than 104!

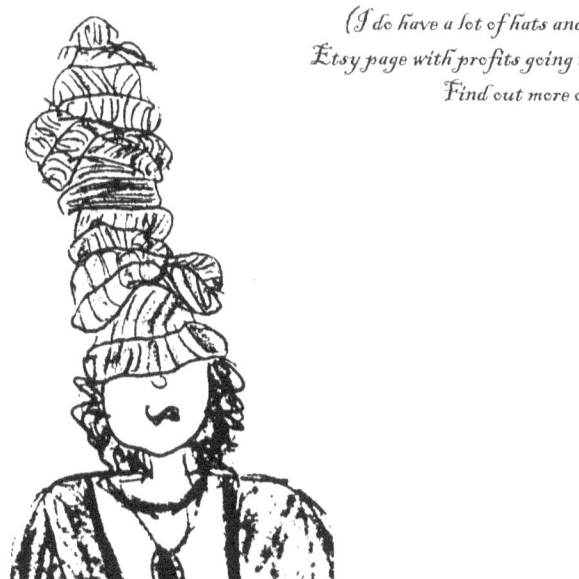

(I do have a lot of hats and will be selling them on an Etsy page with profits going to a mental health charity. Find out more on my social media pages.)

D.I.Y. Disaster Zone

When my beloved says he has a plan,
To prove he is a real handy man.
He's in B & Q getting just the right bit.
I'm in the chemist getting a first aid kit.

I shouldn't complain, but yet again…

He's a D.I.Y. disaster zone,
a D.I.Y. disaster zone.
When he wants to make a change to our family home
He's a D.I.Y. disaster zone.

I dread the days when he gets out his tool,
With a determined look that says he is no fool
I try to smile and support my guy,
But health and safety are in short supply.

It is wrong to complain, but yet again…

He's a D.I.Y. disaster zone,
a D.I.Y. disaster zone.
When he wants to make a change to our family home
He's a D.I.Y disaster zone.

He's keen to prove he's a D.I.Y. master,
But we soon reach for a sticking plaster.
I just hope he finishes in time for tea,
And we don't get a trip to the A and E.

I shouldn't complain, but yet again…

He's a D.I.Y. disaster zone,
a D.I.Y. disaster zone,
When he wants to make a change to our family home

He's a D.I.Y. disaster zone.
He's a D.I.Y. disaster zone,
a D.I.Y. disaster zone,

When he wants to make a change to our family home
He's a D.I.Y disaster zone.

(Sang in the style of a Country and Western hoedown.)

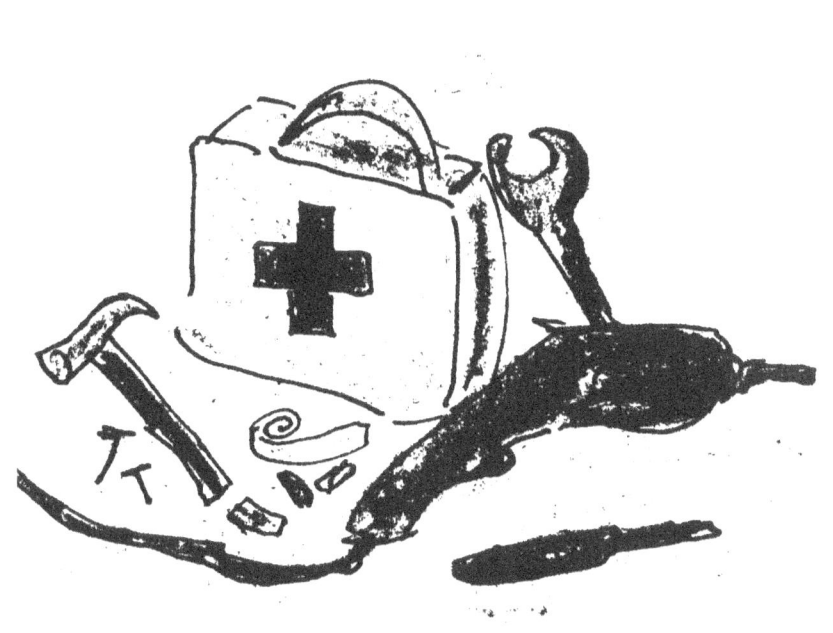

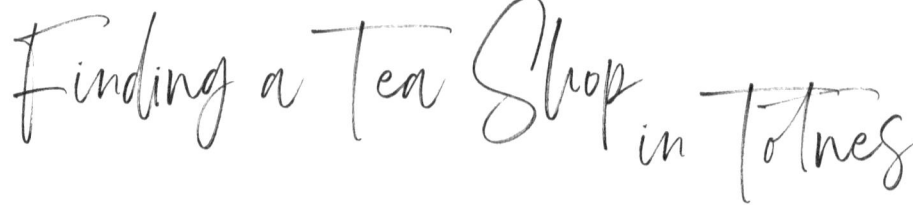

Finding a Tea Shop in Totnes

I want a cup of tea.
Please

Not in a cardboard or plastic cup – I do have standards…
A mug will do … nothing fancy.
I just want a cup of tea.

No … I'm not the mood for Earl Grey at the moment
But thank you for asking…
No … not Lady Grey either or Darjeeling.
No … definitely not Roobush or Camomile –
Which is an acquired taste … I have yet to acquire…
No not Assam or Chai … doesn't need to be green,
And not that Lapsang Souchong … which tastes like an ashtray to me.
I Just want a cup of tea.

No not herbal … I would have said,
Not Raspberry Leaf, Ginger, Peppermint, or one called Fred!
No not coffee – latte – mocha –chino, cappuccino … babycino or cheeky chino… or whatever chino!
Just a nice cup of tea.
I just want a cup of tea.

In a proper cup or mug.
With a small drop of milk … Please?
Thank you.

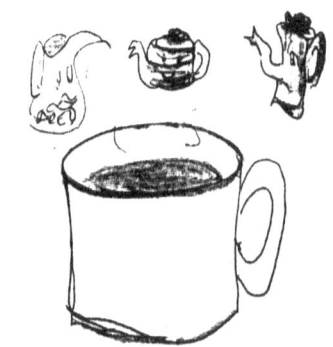

… just one more thing…
Can you make it a decaff please?

(If you have ever visited Totnes in Devon, you will know exactly what I mean.)

Ode To an Unborn Baby

A special moment shared between just us two.
You inside – wriggling, tickling, thumping,

No one else can feel it, Just me.

I watch the movement glide across
The expanse of flesh protruding from
Beneath my rib cage.

Haven't seen my stomach – except
In reflection for a while now.

A special moment – first a fluttering
Then a stampede – little feet, hands
And body in a dance of liberation
In a bubble of fluid.

A special moment – I must remember this.
As we move on to the next stage

And you are finally in my arms.

The No Sleep Baby Blues

I hear my baby crying,
I know just what she needs,
But it's three o'clock in the morning,
And I'm on two hourly feeds!
I got the no sleep baby blues,
Is that what I choose,
The no sleep baby blues.

Some say it's better with a bottle,
Others say it's the breast,
It doesn't seem to matter that much,
When your baby don't want to rest!
Because of the no sleep baby blues.
Is that what we choose,
The no sleep baby blues.

I look to my partner,
He's fast asleep,
Totally oblivious to the crying
And enjoying a slumber deep!
Whilst I have the no sleep baby blues.
Is that what I choose.
The no sleep baby blues.

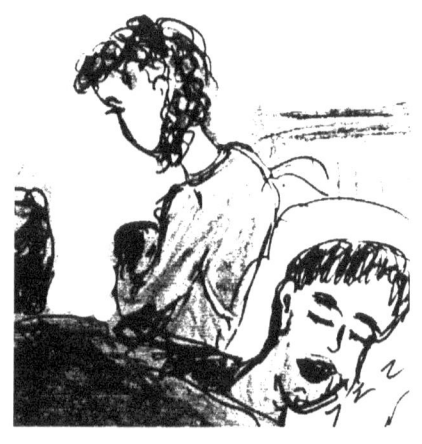

(To a typical blues backing – when I perform it, I get the audience to provide this.)

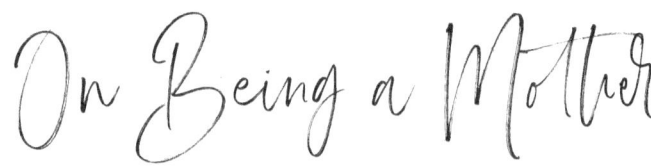

On Being a Mother

It's the moment when…
Your fluffy little head
Rests against my shoulder
A beautiful golden mop that defies any hairbrush

It's the moments when…
You grab my hand and decide,
We should dance around the kitchen,
Rather than get the supper ready.

It's the moments when…
You 'help' with the washing up,
And break a plate,
With a little "Sorry mummy" that you really mean.

It's the moments looking back…
Nearly two and a half years ago…

The difficult birth
The exhaustion
The number of hospital staff surrounding me and my loved ones.
The fear I may not see you after feeling you move inside for so long.
Matched by a flicker of fear in the midwife's eyes.

The tears I could not cry as tiredness engulfed me.
As I tried to keep focussed…

The reassuring squeeze of my hands
From my husband to be and my own mother.

The music - a song I like barely recognised as things became…
A blur…

A young female doctor … tired, joins us.
She's saying something…
– I can barely hear her…

So lost am I…   A machine makes a noise…

Gradually I'm aware of crying louder than my own.
A warm, wet, slightly slimy feeling on my bare belly
        Wriggling – free

You are there…
I'm so tired…
But you are there… At last.
My little boy.
My own, beautiful child.

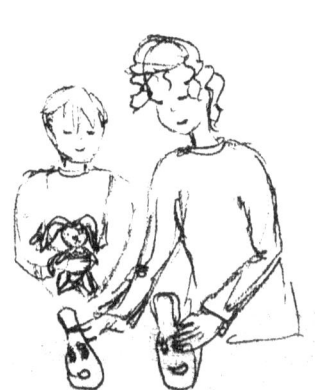

And returning to now.
It's the moments now…

When you look at me with big grey eyes
When you laugh
When you cry
When you dance
When you sing
When you ask for your toy rabbit – whom you have called 'Doodle'.
When you build an impossibly high tower of bricks
When you get frustrated at not being understood
When you draw on the television set
When you roughly fuss the cat and say "Soft"
When you sigh and hug me for no reason
When I help you set up your skittles in the living room
And I hear an unprompted "Thank you mummy" …

The words are like gold on my ears.
But the words are in my heart even stronger.

Thank you my little darling,
Thank you for being.

Thank you for making me your mum.

Promise

A little girl likes to twirl…
Round and round like a ballerina.
"Mummy I'm dancing" she gleefully calls.
I smile in remembrance of another little girl,
Not so dissimilar – with fine golden hair
And a sweet smile.

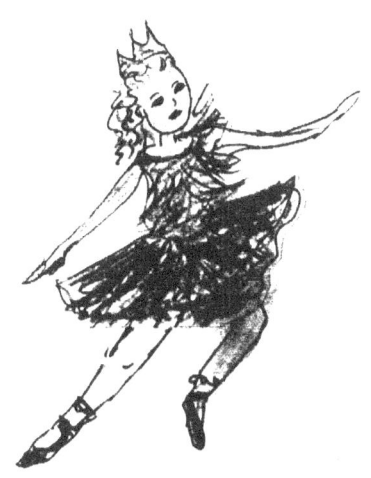

I smile in remembrance and sadness,
Of dreams that couldn't come true.
Well now that has to change,
Whatever dream my little girl has,
I will do all I can to make it happen.

"Mummy! I'm dancing, I'm a ballerina!"
And if that is what she wants to do
So, it shall it be.
My promise to you.

My Christmas

I've got to make a Christmas pudding,
I've got to bake a pie,
I've got to create a Christmas buffet,
Just like my mother would try.

I've got to find the baubles and tinsel,
I've got to find the lights,
This set has little pumpkins on it,
Surely that's, not right?

I've got to wear a Christmas jumper,
I've got to try and smile,
I've got to keep it all together,
Just for a little while.

I've got to get the kids some presents,
I've got to wrap them well,
I've got to make the house feel festive,
Despite the funny smell…

I've got to eat mince pies forever,
(Of which, I am just fine)
I've got to sing the praise of sprouts,
(But that's easy for me and mine).

I've got to make this Christmas season,
Seem happy, bright and gay…
And I've got to keep my sanity,
At least 'til New Year's Day.

I've got to send the cards and gifts,
To make sure they arrive on time.
But I hope you don't think I'm complaining…
For I love Christmas Time!

No Regrets

You seem to spend your life… Wondering.
Asking "What if…"

Yet you never do anything about it.
Why?

Why ask such questions?
And to nobody?

Ask nobody and nobody answers.
So why spend your life wondering…

Don't ask "What if…"
Find out…
Explore…
Discover for yourself.

And ask no more.

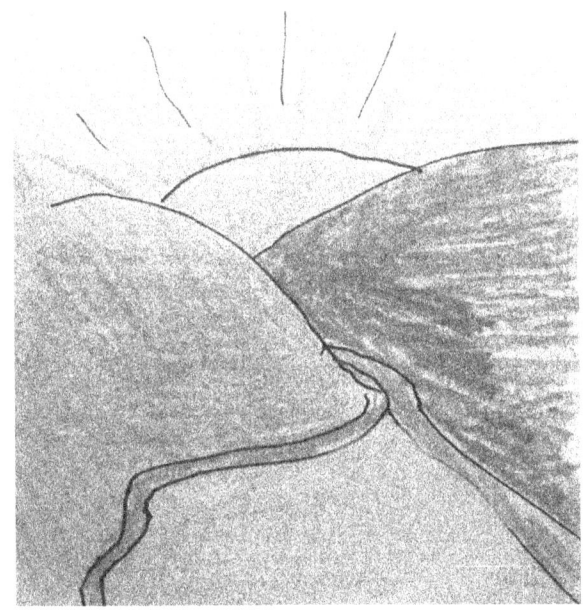

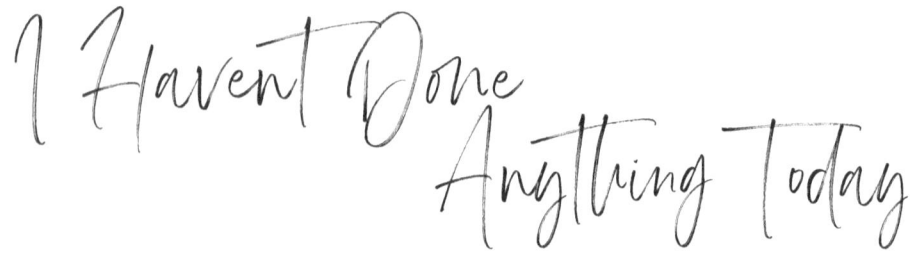

I Haven't Done Anything Today

I've washed the dishes … Tackled some laundry.
Fed the children … Took them tidily to school.

I haven't done anything today.

I've helped a friend on Facebook … Prevented a suicide,
Located and repaired a lost toy … Called in on an invalid.

I haven't done anything today.

I made all the beds … put clothes in a drawer.
Dusted all the shelves … twice, just to be sure.

I haven't done anything today.

I went to get the shopping … Put it away.
Made some food … For tea today.

I haven't done anything today.

I cleaned the muddy footprints … That covered the floor.
Repaired the loose handle … On the Bathroom door.

I haven't done anything today.

I've collected the children … Stopped one of their wars.
Made sure they washed well … And their supper was warm.

I haven't done anything today.

I tidied the living room … Vacuumed it too.
Put the kids to bed … Cleaned the loo.
I haven't done anything today.

I've emptied the bins … Recycled with care.
Realised that I hadn't … Washed my hair…

I haven't done anything today.

Then you return home … To house just the same.
Nothing really altered … Since earlier that day.

And you say quite simply.

"I see you haven't done anything today…"

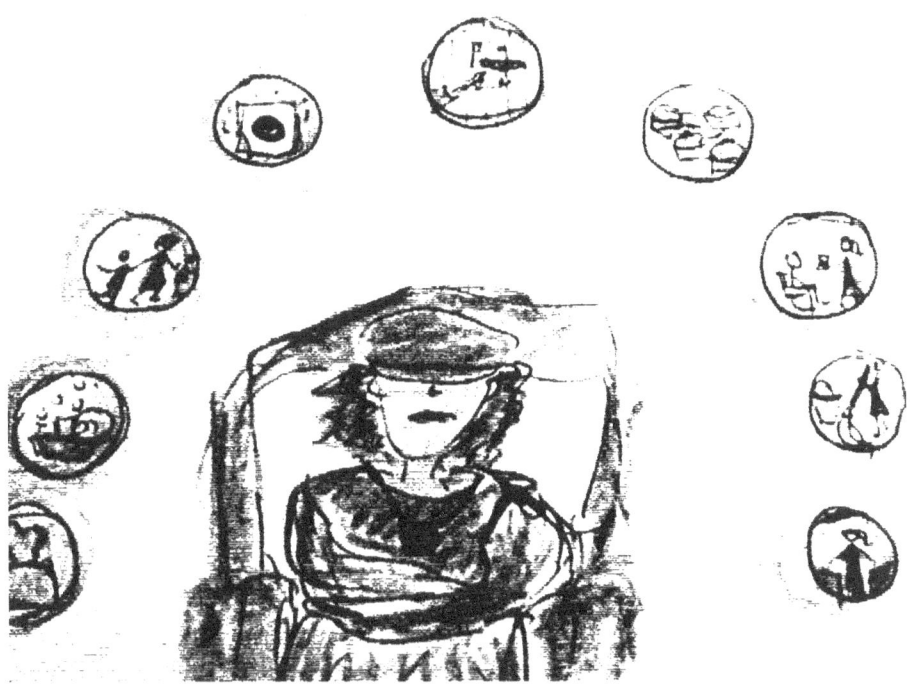

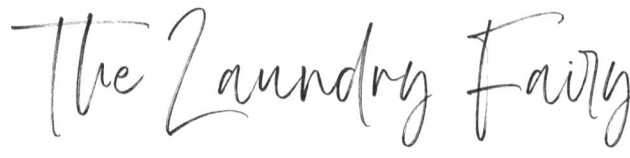

The Laundry Fairy

There is a little fairy, a laundry fairy.
Others believe in her, so she must be true.
She picks up all the dirty shirts and pants,
The P.E. kit and smelly socks hidden from view.

She gathers up all the dirty washing,
Abandoned around the family home.
And takes it to a magic place,
Where many men fear to roam

You never notice that strange item,
Known as a whirring washing machine.
All you know is that your filthy clothes,
Will reappear, fresh and clean.

Of course, she can be a little careless...
Clothes left in a basket or on the stairs,
But most of the time it appears neatly folded,
Ready to wear again, with no cares.

That lovely laundry fairy knows just what magic to do.
To get the washing clean and dry, a blessing to me and you.
Can't understand why our mum doesn't believe in her?
I wonder why she doesn't think it's true?

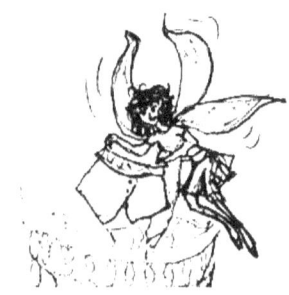

Try Not To Scratch

I find it hard to admit, that finding a nit
In your hair at my age is a great embarrassment.
Being a mature mum can be lots of fun,
But not when your 7-year-old brings the little bitey blighters home.

Being nearly fifty and getting out the 'nitty-gritty' …
Comb to try and move the scratchy little bastards on.
I've recently had a perm, now I try not to squirm …
But pursuing the little gits plays havoc with your hair.

I am constantly feeling the need to …twitch…
And really can't escape the need to … bitch?
As the feeling of the teeny creepy crawly insect feet
Tap dance across my head.

Put on some smelly shampoo,
And hope that that will do.
Attempt to rescue my locks,
And be grateful they are not in my socks.

Like those from world war one,
As testing as the gun,
Fired way too close for comfort.
When comfort was scarce anyhow.

Although the invasion of my hair
Really doesn't compare,
Too the hellish things the soldiers endured,
It's a sure-fire way to experience a moment of history.

All they could do to make them stop,
Was to burn them until they 'pop'...
The little creepy crawly scritchy-scratchy invaders
In their own clothes.

'Pop' them once or twice
Get some relief from the lice,
Infestation, manifestation
Damage to health and to the lice itself.

So, although today's nit is becoming a bit...
Of an annoyance and an irritation to us all.
At least that git of a nit, will finally quit,
Eventually...And leave us alone once more.

Now just to feel the creepy crawly critter
Spread its little bit of bitter...
Bitey, flighty, slightly ... scritchy, scratchy, scritch
Causing a twitch and fighting the urge
To scratch that itch!

(Admit it... you scratched your head during this one...)

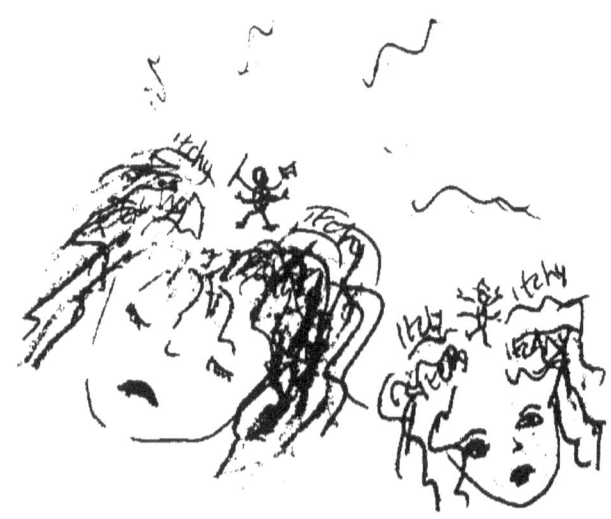

Applause

So, my beloved has cleaned the sink today,
Now he is waiting for his applause.
Took him three hours to remove the stink, he says,
Time for his applause…

Really?
Three hours to clean a sink – wow, what an achievement…
What an achievement to have three hours to spare to clean a stinking sink.
Three hours to do one chore.

He didn't have time for anymore.

Yet I'm expected to this and more.
When twenty-four hours just isn't enough.

Where is my applause?

Where is my award for tackling the many insufferable chores, tedious bores?
That dominate my day, every day.

Where is my applause for ensuring the children are happy and well?
As they work and play.

Where is my applause?
For listening and providing words of comfort as relate your pain,
With absolutely no interest in hearing mine.

Where is my applause?

For food in the cupboard, on the table, in your stomach…
Without any time to play.
The trash taken out… the mess … taken away.

I hear no applause, not for a single thing I do.
Not from your family, especially not from you.
But you cleaned the sink, well done, move on.
Here's your applause …

As yet again… for me… I hear none.

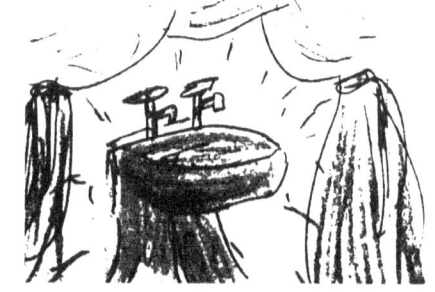

Illusions

Illusions of the future
Delusions of the past.
Time goes so quickly.
Dreams go so fast.
The only real solution
The one that should be…
Is for peace, kindness, love throughout all humanity.

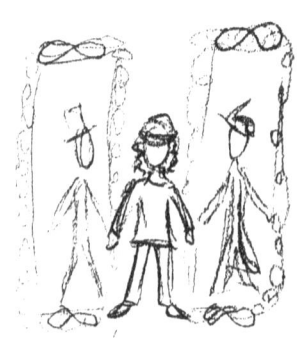

Hazel Eyes

We don't have a lot in common, you and I
Me down in the dumps – mentally and physically
Whilst you are flying high.

Someone I barely noticed until you took part in a show.
I show I loved and then curiosity began to grow.
Who are you? Who are you really?
I decided I needed to know.

We don't have a lot in common, you and I
Similar age – but that's by the by
And not close enough to share a birthday.

Similar backgrounds – but you were loved and revered,
When I said what I wanted to do – my lot decided I was weird.
We both took what opportunities that we could find,
Sadly, most of mine were too few and unkind.

We don't have a lot in common, you and I
You are considered handsome and I ...
Well, some people once said nice things about my chestnut hair and
hazel eyes.

A very long time ago though.

And my eyes, they haven't really changed…
More tired looking but still going through their daily range.
Grey to green to blue to a sort of curious brown – hard to define,
Apparently, something to do with the light.
Apparently, something to do with having hazel eyes.

We don't have a lot in common, you and I
Your success for all to see ... mine hidden unless you pry.

My eyes are what define me and my family,
So-called 'experts' say it's quite rare to see.
I didn't think they were that unusual, personally.
All I know is they are more open as I set out on my journey.

We don't have a lot in common, you and I
Our present circumstances so different, mine especially awry

I am down here, stuck in social housing, you up there, somewhere…
We'll probably never even meet.
Not at a party, show or even in the street.

So instead, I read about you, very interesting it is too.
You've certainly worked hard at the job you chose to do.

We don't have a lot in common, you and I
I feel I have wasted my life, whereas your career is sky high.

You've gained a lot of reward, which you are happy to share.
I like that ... it shows you really do care.
Something that appeals to this hazel eyed girl,
With the once chestnut hair.

But dreams take work in order to come true,
And despite reading to distraction – I don't know the real you.

We don't have a lot in common, you and I
A pleasant diversion but one I must resign.

So, I'll just carry on with the journey,
That I've set myself to achieve.
It's hard, but I'm sure I'll succeed,
if I can just believe... In myself.

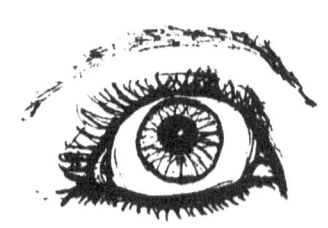

We don't have a lot in common, you and I
But there is one thing I dare to ask you,
Before I quietly say goodbye.

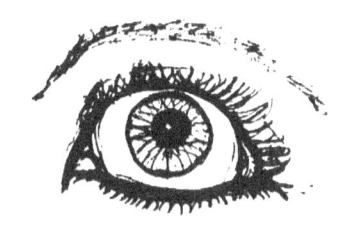

So, I tweet - "What colour are your eyes?"

An unexpected, one-word reply.   "Hazel."

Maybe we're not so different after all ... I just have to try.

Super-bra and Wonder-knickers

With my super-bra and wonder-knickers
I can take on the world.
With a super-bra and wonder-knickers
I feel like a stronger girl.

Reinforced underwear, may not be clothes I can put on in a rush,
But at least in the photographs, I won't need an airbrush.

With my super-bra and wonder-knickers
I start to feel like a real star.
With my super-bra and wonder-knickers
I really feel that I can go far.

They make me feel confident, sassy, lithe - Twenty years young.
Ready to party, celebrate and have some fun.

With my super-bra and wonder-knickers
I am sure I can take on the world.
With my super-bra and wonder-knickers
I'm certain I'm a stronger girl.

But that is not all, oh no, don't forget there's the dress,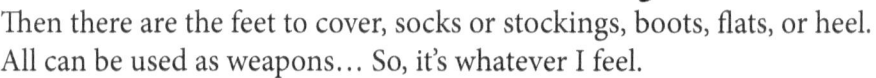
Or whatever I feel is necessary to fight on and impress.

With my super-bra and wonder-knickers
I feel I can issue a battle cry.
With my super-bra and wonder-knickers
Don't mess with me, don't even try.

Then there are the feet to cover, socks or stockings, boots, flats, or heel.
All can be used as weapons… So, it's whatever I feel.

With my super-bra and wonder-knickers
You will see me take on the world.
With my super-bra and wonder-knickers
Don't even mess with this girl.

Hair to style, make-up if I so choose to cover up the emotional scars.
To show that … I don't intend …To lose.

With my super-bra and wonder-knickers
I have my armour to take on the night.
With my super-bra and wonder-knickers
I am more than ready for the fight.

A fight against a world with expectations to conform.
A fight against those who define and establish the 'norm'.

My super-bra and wonder-knickers
Hold me tight, refine my shout.
Without super-bra and wonder-knickers
… can I ever just let it all out?

Speed Dating

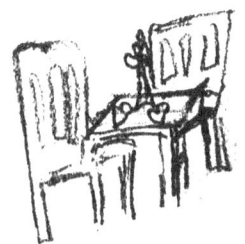

So here I am, A newly single mum of two.
Not exactly all that defines me - But it'll do.
Some friends suggested I go on a date,
Find 'someone special' before it's too late.

Thanks 'friends' if that is what you are.
I thought I was doing well thought I was shining like a star.
But my 'friends' are quite persuasive so here I am in a shabby hotel.
Surrounded by the desperation brigade and things are not going well.

First, we're told to mingle, we have been given a free drink.
But frankly it's not that appealing and the majority of them stink.
The 'ladies' are sat at tables, the 'fair blooms' should be approached.
With caution in my opinion – the men circle ready to be reproached.

The first one is called Gary and he really likes his car.
He promises to drive me wherever I want to go - so long as it has a bar.
The second one is 'Mikey' – he went to university you know.
Although he didn't quite manage to finish – but is quite happy on the dole.

The next one is quite exotic – Julio is his name.
He looks around, boredom in his eyes, so in some ways we are the same.
But the charms of dashing Julio are limited, he sweats more than a bull.
And as he talks about his successes it's the clear the comparison is full….

Then I'm introduced to Arthur, he calls himself 'a proper gent'.
He shows off a fake Rolex, and that's not all that's bent.
Sebastian seems quite nice; he admits he doesn't have a lot to say.
His beloved wife brought him along – apparently, they like 'role play'.
Oliver seems very shy – he admits it's not his scene,
I wonder if his mother knows he is out – far too young and green.
Milo is a chef you know, cooking is his passion,
And lots of pretty young girls too, especially those into fashion.

There are more men than women here, we're expected to be polite.
I secretly wish I were elsewhere, being more productive with my night.
I finally think of something to speed things up and end this silly game.
I look deeply into their eyes and say, "Are you Brexit or Remain?"

Queen of Procrastination

I'm the Queen of Procrastination
Always looking for a distraction
To help me avoid the task in hand.
I set out a well-meaning plan.
A project that I know I can…
Complete, if I just sit and… and…

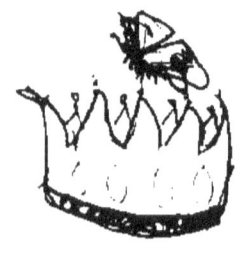

Oh, look at that pretty butterfly – how did that get in here?

I Am the Star

Hearing the over forty something's taking apart a soap opera.
I wonder if they see the story going on in front of their eyes.
Watching the people walking by desperate for somewhere to go.
Not wanting the responsibility of starring in their own show.

I see faces whirling past in a cinematic blur,
And the look on peoples' faces, anxiously saying "what is it worth,
What is it worth, what is worth?"

They say life is a movie story worthy of any famous award.
What do we need now to take the bow and say I am the star?
I am the Star. I AM THE STAR of my own show…

His story could be written down. Her story could be more profound.
Costumes - set and action - chosen to suit the crowd.
The extras walking through your life - Some give joy, some give strife,
Filling days with black and white - And many shades of grey.

Script change happens when it's least expected to.
That's just part of the drama. The house could burn, the lottery won but
what is it worth, what is it worth, what is it worth?

They say life is a movie story worthy of any famous award.
What do we need now to take the bow and say I am the star?
I am the Star. I AM THE STAR of my own show!

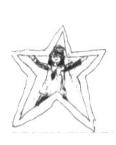 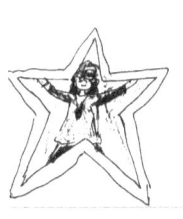 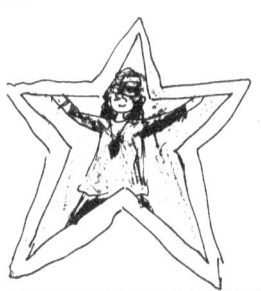

Waking Up Before The Alarm

I'm having a lovely dream.
I'm working in a theatre.
The Actor, Hugh Jackman is there.
He is selling popcorn, I'm selling programmes.
We are having a laugh.

The audience are safely in the auditorium.
I'm free to do what I want.
So, I wander…I wander and take in the atmosphere.
It is exhilarating.

Then my wanderings turn into a search for the toilets.
Each time I find one there is something wrong.
It's broken or in the wrong place.

I recognise this aspect of the dream.
It's the one I always have, and I'm sure I'm not the only one,
When my bladder nudges into my subconscious.
"Hey … Wake up … we have an urgent need!"

So, I reluctantly submerge from my colourful dream state,
Into a world of darkness.
The electric light guides me as I wander to the toilet … the real one
And take the necessary call of nature.
Getting back into the sanctuary of my snuggly bed

I check the time on my phone.
(Yes, I know you shouldn't keep it by the bed but…)
It is exactly one hour before my alarm will go off.
Not exactly an ideal situation.

Thanks bladder… thanks for nothing.
Thanks for interrupting my much-desired sleep.
Thanks for interrupting my beautiful dream.
You could have woken me with a good four or five hours to spare.
I could have enjoyed a new dream by then.
Or why didn't you wake me seconds before the alarm.
That would've been reasonable.

Still, I have just under an hour to rest - I'll take that.

I settle down again and try to revisit the theatre dream.
But it's not the same. It's too artificial.
And Hugh Jackman has disappeared.
I lie awake…looks like the sky is getting a bit lighter.
The birds are certainly beginning to make their presence known.

Maybe I should just get up? Like any sensible person would do.
Start the day a little earlier. Get things done – without a rush.
Nah … not for me. Have never been particularly sensible,
Why should I start now when my bed feels so good?

I check the time again.
48 minutes until the alarm goes off.
I'll take that.

So, I settle down again, but the desire for sleep is still not satisfied.
My phone buzzes…I don't usually hear it as I'm usually still asleep.
I discover it's my friend posting a picture,
On a social media platform, I'll look and like it later.

My friend lives in California.
I mentally work out the time delay.
She would be preparing to go to go to bed soon.
Funny to think she is about to sleep when I'm about to wake.
Well … soon … ish…

The birds are really getting their volume up now.
It is definitely getting lighter.
I can see the colour of the curtains.
They are purple.

I check my phone again.
30 minutes until the alarm.
I'll take that.

So, I settle down again, all chance of a decent dream gone.
Maybe I'll try meditation.
How does it go again?

"Imagine descending a staircase...
Count backwards slowly ... 10,9,8..." I'm bored already.

I should get up. It's definitely getting lighter.
Curtain more of a light blue now.
The birds are really giving it their all.
A chaotic cacophony to a brand-new day

Or a racket because a seagull has joined in.
I Wonder what time it is…
I check my phone once again.

Ten minutes to the alarm... I'll take that.
I suppose it'll have to do.
Certainly, don't feel like getting up just yet.

Anyhow – there is always the snooze button.

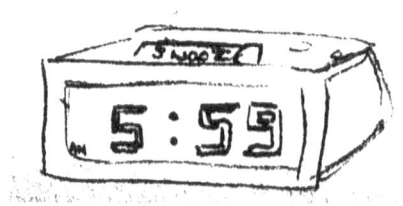

I've Grown Up

Looking through old papers
One thing springs to mind…
I've grown up.

I can't quite describe how it happened.
I can't quite decide the when and where.
It took it's time… But it's there.

I don't feel so scared anymore.
Every day presents it's challenges…
Like some merchant displaying his wares…

But the choice is mine and I can handle it.
I've read a lot. I've seen a lot.
I've been places. I've clutched at straws.

I don't need anything now, just a roof over my head,
A chance to realise my dreams, my way.
A cup of milk and a book at bedtime

I've grown up. No tears and tantrums.
Everything clear and precise.
A refreshing perspective on life.

I've grown up… Acknowledging the child that I am.

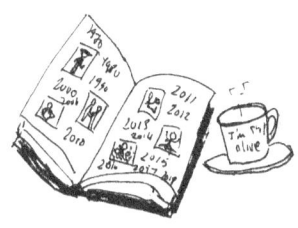

A Faint Smell of Cabbages

Today I caught the number 12 bus.

Nothing unusual in that.
I do it at least once a week.
After a round of charity shops and coffee stops
I was ready to go home.

A far more matured lady got on in front of me.
She was very chatty,
she wanted to give me her life story.

I didn't mind…
Although it was clear that it was going to be a very long one.

As she was telling her glorious tale
Of adventures far and wide…
I became a bit distracted,
By a faint smell of cabbages.

It reminded me of the old people's home I once visited.
When my own grandmother was imprisoned there,
First her body, then her mind.
Trapped in a bed she could barely move from.

Age has a mean trick of sneaking up on you.
You look in the mirror, to see the face of a happy go lucky 19-year-old,
You feel the same inside…

But the mirror shows a very different story.
You start to look like your mother.

Another glance... Your grandmother
Where has the time gone.

The children that surround you keep you feeling young,
Until you realise, they are the children,
Of the children, of the children you once knew.

Time is so cruel.

This lady on the bus definitely had a faint smell of cabbages.
It followed me home.

Then I look in the mirror and begin to realise.
The faint smell of cabbages…

Is mine too.

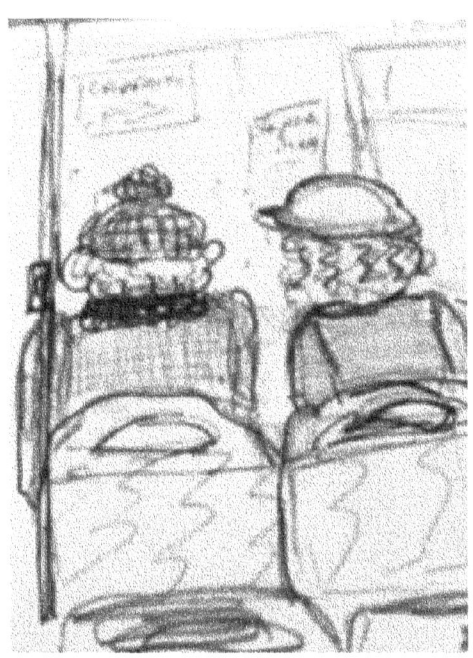

Ageing Well

Some say age is just a number,
As you move further from the date,
You first breathed air upon this earth.
And stumbled towards your fate.

Some say age is just a state of mind.
"You're only as old as you feel".
The emotional rollercoaster plays a part,
There are days the aches and pain are very real.

Some say age is something you just have to accept,
The alternative won't let you thrive.
Whatever life decides to throw your way,
You just have to do what you can to survive.

Some say age is a journey, not a destination.
If you are lucky you find the map.
If you are really lucky you find a guide
Someone at your side, who has your back.

Ageing is pretty inevitable,
It can be good to watch those numbers swell.
Whatever you do, just hope to be true,
To your heart and keep ageing well.

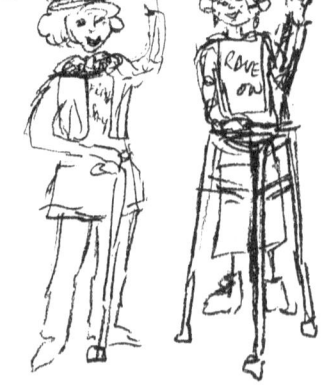

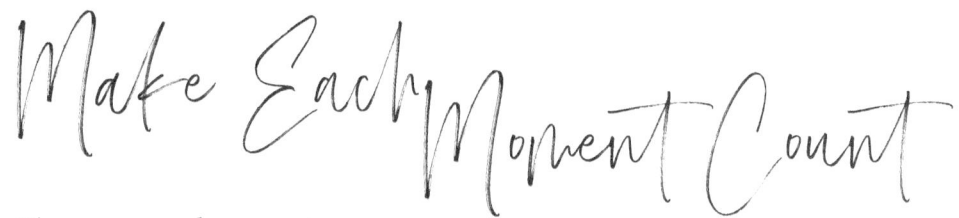

Make Each Moment Count

There are good moments.
There are bad moments.
There are 'bleagh' moments.
But moments there will be.
You can't stop them.
It's the very nature of time.

Moments lined up to be counted.
Here's one coming up now ...
There it goes ... did you enjoy it?

If not, why not?
Were you not paying it enough attention?

I'll send you another one.
Here it comes ... watch it fly...
And ... fly away.

That was nice wasn't it?

I gave you that moment.
You could say it wasn't mine to give,
But I'm the one standing up here in front of you.

I gave you that moment as a gift,
It's up to you to decide how you receive it.
How you want to spend it.

It's the same with all the other moments.
You can't stop them coming...
You can't stop time...

Well, time will stop for you at some point,
For everyone.

But that's not a moment you want to rush towards.

Time trickles along
With precious moments like a gently flowing stream
As you observe the pictures, papers, plans,
And the moments spent on creating your dreams.

Then you realise how much you have achieved…
Or not as the case may be.
Saying goodbye to well-meant schemes.

Suddenly there seems to be a lot less time ahead.

More moments in the past then in the future…

Time can be a real bastard sometimes…

That's why we should make each moment count.

Those hazy, crazy, beautiful moments
The ones to cherish, the ones to forget,
There are all there.
They all share the role of making you who you are.

Here's a moment for you… There it goes…

Did you enjoy it?

If not, why not?

It doesn't matter what you thought really.

That moment has gone…

Page 52